get into

KNITTING

learn from scratch and be inspired!

sophie scott

WAYLAND

CONTENTS

GETTING STARTED

Knitting is the art of making loops, called stitches, with a pair of knitting needles and some wool. By moving your needles and the yarn in different ways, you can link all these loops together to make knitted fabric – and then you can create all sorts of things!

This book will show you how to complete eight fantastic knitting projects – each one will show you a new technique to practise, and includes a fun twist for you to try once you've mastered the skill. If you ever get stuck, there's a help section at the back.

Don't worry if you feel a bit clumsy holding the needles and yarn at first – it will get a lot easier over time. Focus on following the instructions, and soon you'll be holding the needles very comfortably!

Once you've picked up some essentials from a craft shop (see pages 4–5), you'll be ready to start knitting!

EQUIPMENT

You'll be able to find all the following things in any good knitting or haberdashery shop.

YARN Yarn can be made from wool, alpaca, cotton or acrylic fibres – and sometimes it may be a mix. Wool is easiest to work with. Of course, always pick your favourite colours!

Each yarn has a different thickness, and each has a size of needle that matches it. Check the yarn's label to make sure you are buying the correct needles for your knitting project.

KNITTING NEEDLES
Knitting needles come in different materials, such as bamboo, plastic and metal. You may find bamboo needles easier at first, since these are not as slippery as metal or plastic needles.

SCISSORS Smaller ones are best for snipping little threads and trimming pompoms.

TAPESTRY NEEDLE This is a special type of sewing needle with a large hole – called an 'eye' – to fit yarn through, and a blunt tip so the yarn doesn't split.

TAPE MEASURE This is important when checking you are making things the right size.

SEWING NEEDLE AND THREAD A sewing needle is thinner and sharper than a tapestry needle. Use it with thread to sew pieces of knitting together.

SEWING PINS AND SAFETY PINS These hold everything in place when sewing your knitting together.

DECORATIVE EXTRAS Felt, buttons, googly eyes, sequins, ribbon ... whatever you want to add!

CUSHION PAD A bag filled with stuffing that you can use inside a cushion cover.

GLUE Fabric glue is best, but you can always use a blob of PVA glue if you have it.

FABRIC GLUE

PVA

BASIC BOOKMARK STAGE 1

CASTING ON

This first project covers all the basics of knitting, and you'll have a useful bookmark at the end! Before you start using knitting stitches, you must 'cast on' a row of stitches to work from.

STEP 1

The first part of casting on is to make a slip-knot – a special loop that counts as your first stitch. Twist the end of your yarn (called the 'tail') into a circle, with the tail end lying on top. Fold the tail end in half and pull the folded part through the back of the circle.

STEP 2

Place your slip-knot on to one of your needles and pull the tail so the loop is snug. Hold this needle in your left hand and the other needle in your right hand.

YOU WILL NEED

50 g of DK yarn

Scissors

Tapestry needle

Pair of 4-mm needles

Sometimes the 'front' or 'back' of your knitting work will be mentioned. When you hold your needles, imagine a line along the top splitting them in half. The side facing you is the front, and the side facing away from you is the back.

STEP 3

Hold the yarn in your right-hand fingers, behind the needles. Insert the tip of your right-hand needle into the slip-knot. Check that the needles make an 'X', with the left-hand needle sitting on top.

STEP 4

Going from left to right, wrap the yarn around the tip of the right-hand needle, making a little bridge over the top. Make sure you use the yarn coming from the ball, not the tail end!

STEP 5

Slowly slide the right-hand needle back until the tip has come out under the loop on the left needle. You are aiming to 'catch' the little bridge that you just made so it sits as a loop on the right-hand needle.

STEP 6

Insert the tip of your left-hand needle into the new loop so it sits next to the slip-knot.

STEP 7

Now remove the right-hand needle from the loop.

STEP 8

Place your right-hand needle tip in between the two stitches, then repeat steps 4–7. Do this until you have 10 stitches. That will be the width of your bookmark!

BASIC BOOKMARK STAGE 2

KNIT STITCH

Now that you have cast on, you have a foundation to build upon. Even though the hobby itself is called knitting, there is also a type of stitch called 'knit stitch'. This is how you do it.

STEP 1

Hold the needle with the stitches in your left hand and the bare needle in your right hand. Hold the yarn with your right-hand fingers.

STEP 2

Just as when casting on, place the tip of your right-hand needle into the first stitch, making an 'X' with your needles – the left-hand needle should be on top.

STEP 3

With your right hand, wrap the yarn around the tip of the right-hand needle from left to right, making a bridge over the top of the right-hand needle.

STEP 4

Just as when casting on, slide the right-hand needle back so the tip pokes out from under the loop you entered, then slide it on top of the left-hand needle, bringing the wrapped-around yarn with it.

STEP 5

By sliding right with your right-hand needle, guide the original first stitch up to the end of your left-hand needle and let it drop off. You have now knitted one stitch!

STEP 6

Continue repeating steps 2–4 until every stitch has moved to the right-hand needle. You have finished a row! Now swap your needles, so you have all the stitches on the left needle and an empty needle in your right hand.

STEP 7

Keep on completing rows of knit stitch until you have a rectangle about 15 cm long.

When your work is made up entirely of knit stitches, you have made a knitting pattern called 'garter stitch'.

BASIC BOOKMARK STAGE 3

CASTING OFF

Once your bookmark is long enough, you'll need to fasten off the stitches so they won't undo. This is called 'casting off'.

STEP 1

Casting off always requires two stitches on your right-hand needle, so start by knitting two stitches.

STEP 2

One of these stitches is now going to 'leap frog' over the other one and drop off the needle. Do this by picking up the first stitch you just knitted with the tip of your left-hand needle.

STEP 3

As you lift the first stitch over the second stitch and off the right-hand needle, hold on to the tail of the yarn with your right hand to make sure the second stitch doesn't jump off too.

STEP 4

Knit one stitch so you once again have two stitches on the right-hand needle and repeat steps 2–3. Keep doing this until you only have one stitch left on the right-hand needle.

STEP 5

Cut the yarn, leaving a long tail of about 20 cm. Loosen the last stitch to make its loop a little bigger, then thread the tail through it, pulling tight.

STEP 6

You will always have tail ends at the start and end of your knitting – and sometimes more if you joined in new yarn. To tidy it, thread a tapestry needle with the tail end and weave the needle in and out of the bumps of knitting on the back side of your fabric. Cut the tail end close to the fabric.

GIFT IT

Bookmarks are perfect for practising basic knitting skills. Make a few in different colours and hand them out as gifts!

MONSTER FINGER PUPPET

This little monster just wants to have fun! In this project you will use some simple sewing to make the puppet shape rather than casting off as normal.

YOU WILL NEED

50 g of DK yarn

Scissors

Tape measure

Sewing pins

Fabric glue

FABRIC GLUE

4-mm knitting needles

Tapestry needle

Bits for decoration: googly eyes, felt, stickers or sequins

STEP 1
Cast on enough stitches to give you a width of 8 cm, then knit until you have a piece that is 6 cm long. Don't cast off. Instead, leaving a length of at least 30 cm for sewing up, cut the tail end of the yarn. Thread a tapestry needle with the long tail.

STEP 2
Using the tip of the tapestry needle, pick up and pass each stitch off the knitting needle and on to the tapestry needle. Keep going until all the stitches are sitting on the tail length of yarn.

STEP 4
Fold the monster in half and pin the edges. Weave your tapestry needle in between the stitches at the edge of your knitting to sew the puppet together – pass the needle through the fabric, not over it.

STEP 3
Pull the tail end of the yarn tight. This will make all the stitches gather together and shape the top of the head.

STEP 6
Now it's time to make your monster come to life! You could try: cutting out some felt teeth shapes and securing with a blob of glue; adding a mouth and eyebrows by sewing details in a different colour; and adding googly eyes (or just one)!

STEP 5
To secure the yarn at the end, keep the last sewing stitch loose. Thread the yarn through this loop and pull tight. Weave in any ends and trim any loose tails of yarn.

ROAR
Try making animal finger puppets instead of monsters!

COSY COWL

A cowl is similar to a scarf, except the ends are joined together to create a circle. This cowl uses toggles.

YOU WILL NEED

2 × 50-g balls of chunky yarn

Scissors

Tape measure

10-mm needles

Tapestry needle

3 toggles

STEP 1
Cast on enough stitches to give you roughly 15 cm of width.

STEP 2
Knit every row. After a while, you will start to run out of yarn from the first ball. Keep an eye on how much you have left – you want to finish the ball at the end of a row, with a leftover strand of at least 10 cm.

STEP 3
To start a new ball, lay the leftover strand of your old yarn on top of the tail end of the new ball. Tie the new yarn around the old yarn with a loose knot. Slide the knot close to your needle.

STEP 4

Leave the tail ends dangling and use the new yarn to continue. Keep knitting until the cowl is long enough to wrap around your neck, plus a bit extra that overlaps. Once it is long enough, cast off and weave in any loose ends.

STEP 5

Sew the toggles on to the cowl using the same yarn: thread it through the toggles a few times and secure it at the back with a double knot.

STEP 6

Poke the toggles through the other end of the fabric to make your cowl a circle.

KNIT ON

If you would prefer to make a scarf, don't sew the ends together, and keep on knitting! (You'll need a couple of extra balls of yarn.)

STRIPY HAND-WARMERS

Stripes are a great way to include all your favourite colours in only one project. Adding stripes uses the same method as joining in a new ball of yarn.

YOU WILL NEED

2 × 50-g balls of DK yarn (each one a different colour)

Scissors

Tape measure

Tapestry needle

4-mm needles

Sewing pins

STEP 1

Measure the width of your hand along your knuckles and cast on a width that is double this size in the first colour (Colour A). Leave a 20-cm-long tail end for sewing up later. Knit two rows in Colour A.

STEP 2

To change colour, lay a 10-cm tail of Colour A on top of the tail of Colour B. Use the Colour B tail to tie a knot, so Colour A is held inside. Slide the knot close to your needle.

STEP 3

Leave the ends of Colour A dangling with the ball of yarn still attached. Now use colour B to knit two rows.

STEP 4

Now swap to Colour A and repeat steps 2–3. Keep knitting two rows of each colour until your piece is large enough to cover from your wrist to your knuckles.

STEP 5

Cast off using either colour, leaving a long tail. Cut the tail of the other colour too, also leaving a tail.

STEP 6

When you make stripes, the sides of your knitting look different. Fold your knitting in half, so the side you don't want to show is on the outside. Pin in place, then put your hand on top to measure where the gap for your thumb should be. Use two coloured pins to mark the gap.

STEP 7

Thread the tapestry needle with the cast-off tail and sew the sides up to the thumb gap. Then thread your needle with the cast-on tail and sew up the other side of the thumb gap. Remove pins, weave in any loose ends, trim them and turn the handwarmer inside out. Repeat all these steps again to complete your pair of handwarmers!

EVEN WARMER

Knit longer rectangles to make funky arm-warmers instead!

ANIMAL HAT

What's better than a hat?
An animal hat with ears,
a nose and a mouth!

YOU WILL NEED

2 × 50-g balls of brown
Aran weight yarn

Tape measure

Sewing
needle and
thread

Tapestry
needle

Scissors

5-mm
needles

2 buttons

Scraps
of felt

Sewing
pins

STEP 1

Measure around your head and then divide this measurement in half. This will be the width of your hat, so cast on enough stitches to equal that width. Make sure you leave a long tail for sewing up later.

STEP 2

Knit enough rows to make a rectangle big enough to cover your head from your forehead to the back, plus 10 cm more, which will be used for making the ears. When it is big enough, cast off, leaving a long tail for sewing up.

STEP 3

Fold the rectangle in half lengthways and pin the sides together. Sew up the two shorter sides using a tapestry needle and the cast-on and cast-off tails. Remove pins, weave in any loose ends and flip the hat inside out so that the seams are hidden.

STEP 4

Cut a length of yarn and wrap it round a corner of the hat a few times to make an ear. Knot the yarn several times.

STEP 5

Thread the ends of the ear yarn with a tapestry needle and sew them through to the inside of the hat. Knot the ends again and trim, then repeat steps 4–5 for the second ear.

STEP 6

Cut shapes from felt to make the mouth and nose. Sew them on using a sewing needle and thread. Use buttons for the eyes – knot the end of some thread, then weave the needle through the hat and the holes of the button. To secure the thread, keep your last stitch loose and pass the needle through it, then pull the thread tight.

GO WILD

With buttons and some felt, you can make any animal you want!

POMPOM

What better way to top off your knitting than with a fluffy pompom? You'll need some to complete the pompom cushion on pages 22–23.

STEP 1

Place the mug on the cardboard and draw around it. Then place the bottle lid in the middle of the circle and draw around that. Cut out the outer and inner circles to create a doughnut shape. Repeat this so you have two.

STEP 2

Wind off a small ball of yarn and wrap the two doughnuts together by going through the hole. Keep going until you can't fit any more yarn through the hole. If you need to add some new yarn, just wind it in.

YOU WILL NEED

Yarn (any thickness)

Scissors

Strong string

Tapestry needle

Thin cardboard

Pencil

Bottle lid

 Mug

When the hole gets very small, thread the yarn on to a needle to help you get the last bit through.

STEP 3

Snip the yarn along the outside of the circle, cutting between the two cardboard doughnuts. Make sure you don't pull any strands of yarn loose.

STEP 4

Wrap some strong string around the pompom several times, in between the cardboard doughnuts. Tie a few knots to make it secure.

STEP 5

Carefully remove the cardboard doughnuts by snipping the cardboard. Give the pompom a little trim with some scissors to tidy the ends. You can cut the string that you used to tie the pompom together, or keep it long for attaching to knitting.

GET FUNKY

Try using more than one colour in your pompom for a multi-coloured look!

POMPOM CUSHION

This pattern uses knit stitch and a new stitch called 'purl'. Purl is like a back-to-front version of knit stitch. When rows of knit and purl take turns, the pattern is called 'stocking stitch'.

YOU WILL NEED

4 pompoms   Scissors

2 × 50-g balls of chunky yarn

Tapestry needle

Sewing pins

Cushion pad

10-mm needles

STEP 1

Measure the width of your cushion pad, then cast on enough stitches to match that width. Knit one row.

STEP 2

The next row will be purl stitch. Insert the right-hand needle into the first stitch from right to left, sliding it on top of the left-hand needle and making sure that the yarn is at the front of your work.

STEP 3

Wrap the yarn anti-clockwise around the right-hand needle, so the yarn now lies on the left-hand side of it, at the front of your work.

STEP 4

Slide the right-hand needle back until it catches the loop you just wrapped, then slide it under the left-hand needle and use it to slip the original stitch off the left needle. That's one purl stitch!

STEP 6

Do one row of knit stitch, then one row of purl stitch. Repeat until you have enough fabric to wrap around your cushion pad, then cast off.

STEP 5

Repeat steps 2–4 until you have moved all the stitches over to the right-hand needle.

STEP 7

Fold the rectangle in half with the knit sides touching and pin. Cut a 30-cm length of yarn and sew down two sides of the cover, leaving one open. Unpin, then flip the cover inside out. Stuff with the cushion pad and sew shut with a long length of yarn.

STEP 8

Use the pompom tails to sew one to each corner of the cushion. Knot securely at the back of the cushion.

DECORATE

Once you've mastered pompoms, try experimenting with stripy patterns or button decorations!

PENCIL CASE

Keep your pens organised with this knitted pencil case! This project uses a 'decreasing' technique, where two stitches are knitted together, gradually making shorter and shorter rows to create the flap.

STEP 1

Cast on a width of 20 cm, then knit enough rows to make a rectangle roughly 15 cm long.

STEP 2

To create the flap of your pencil case, start by inserting the right-hand needle tip into the first two stitches on your left-hand needle.

YOU WILL NEED

Scissors

4-mm knitting needles

50 g of DK yarn

1 button

Tapestry needle

STEP 3

Now continue as if you were making a knit stitch: wrap your yarn around the needle, draw the needle back and catch the new stitch on your right-hand needle. Then guide the old two stitches off the left-hand needle.

STEP 4

Knit across most of the rest of the row, leaving two stitches on your left-hand needle. Knit the last two stitches together as before.

STEP 5

Repeat steps 2–4, knitting two stitches together at the start and end of each row until you have a row that is only two stitches long. Cast off these final stitches.

STEP 6

Sew the cast-off tail back into the tip of the triangle, but don't pull the yarn all the way through – this will be the loop the button will pass through. Sew back and forth in the same spot to secure the loop. Pass the needle through the last stitch, then weave in the ends.

STEP 7

Fold up the rectangle to meet the bottom of the triangle and pin the short sides together. Sew them up with yarn. Remove pins and turn the pencil case inside out.

STEP 8

Place the button on the front of the flap and sew in place with some yarn. Secure it at the back with a double knot.

GO MINI

Start off with a smaller rectangle to make a money purse instead!

BUNTING

Knit a string of flags to decorate your bedroom! In this project you'll learn how to add more stitches to your knitting – this is called 'increasing'.

STEP 1

Cast on two stitches, then knit one (tiny!) row.

STEP 2

Increase the first stitch: start to knit as usual but do not slip the stitch off the left-hand needle.

STEP 3

Insert your right-hand needle into the back loop of the original stitch. Wrap the yarn around the needle and knit the stitch. You should have two stitches on the right-hand needle.

YOU WILL NEED

50 g of DK yarn

Scissors

Sewing needle and thread

Tapestry needle

4-mm knitting needles

1 m x 1-cm-wide ribbon

STEP 4
Repeat steps 2–3 to increase the second stitch on your needle in the same way. You will have four stitches on your needle. Knit one row.

STEP 5
Now do another increase row: increase the first stitch, knit across most of the row as normal, and increase the last stitch. Knit the rest of the triangle by alternating a knit row with an increase row.

STEP 6
When you have 20 stitches on the needle, cast off.

STEP 7
Repeat steps 1–6 to make five flags. Then weave in their ends and attach them to a length of ribbon using a sewing needle and thread.

GETTING DOTTY
Try using ribbon in a matching colour, but with a funky dotted pattern, to create a different look.

WHEN KNITTING GOES WRONG

Don't panic if you make a mistake when knitting – there is always a way to fix it. Check your knitting every row or two to make sure everything is on track. As you practise, you'll get used to spotting when something doesn't look right – and will have the confidence to fix it!

HOW TO UNDO A KNIT STITCH

STEP 1
For each stitch you need to undo, look for the loop directly under the stitch on the needle. Stretch out your knitting to find the right loop.

STEP 2
Pick up this loop by entering it with your left-hand needle.

STEP 3
Drop the stitch off the right-hand needle. Pull the yarn gently to undo the stitch.

To undo a purl stitch, use the same method, but hold your yarn at the front.

ELP! I KEEP ADDING STITCHES

Your last stitch from the previous row may have twisted around to look like two stitches, so make sure there is a single loop sat on the left-hand needle.

Take care not to split the yarn with your right-hand needle, as this can make multiple stitches.

HELP! I HAVE MYSTERY HOLES

- If you wrap yarn around the needle *before* entering a stitch, you can accidentally make a little hole in your work. Follow the instructions on the left-hand page for undoing stitches.

- Check you have not dropped a stitch.

- Holes are sometimes made by picking up extra stitches, so check whether your knitting is getting wider.

ELP! MY KNITTING IS REALLY TIGHT

If you are pulling the yarn very firmly after each stitch, the loops on your needle will be very small. Loosen up and try holding your yarn differently.

When you wrap a stitch, make sure you are wrapping around the largest part of your needle, not the tip. Wrapping around the thin tip will make smaller stitches.

NEXT STEPS

Now you've learned all the essential steps of knitting, why not try to design your own projects? Graph paper is useful to help you plan your pattern – you can use each square to equal one stitch.

It's always more fun to knit with others – perhaps you could start a knitting group at school?

A teacher or person from your local community might be able to show you new techniques. Once you have learned knit and purl there are lots of different ways to combine them to make different patterns.

USEFUL WEBSITES

Ravelry
www.ravelry.com
This knitting and yarn database is free to use. Many of the patterns are also free to download.

Knitting Help
www.knittinghelp.com
Free patterns and videos to help you with knitting techniques.

Knitty
www.knitty.com
Free online knitting magazine with tutorials and patterns.

Loop
www.loopknitting.com
Knitting shop that stocks yarns and haberdashery, and ships all over the world.

GLOSSARY

CASTING OFF Binding off knitting securely so that the stitches won't unravel.

CASTING ON Creating the foundation row of stitches that will start a piece of knitting.

GARTER STITCH Fabric that is bumpy on both sides, made by knitting every row.

HABERDASHERY Shop that sells small items used in sewing, such as needles and thread.

RIGHT SIDE The side of your knitting that will be on show. Often this is where the pattern will look best.

SEAM A line where two pieces of knitting have been sewn together.

SLIP-KNOT A special loop that becomes the first stitch when casting on.

STOCKING STITCH A type of fabric that is smooth on one side and bumpy on the other, made by alternating rows of knit and purl.

WEAVING IN ENDS Sewing any tail ends of your work back into the knitting so it is neatly finished.

WRONG SIDE The side of the knitting that will be hidden from view when the project is complete.

INDEX

Published in Great Britain in 2018 by Wayland

Copyright © Wayland, 2016

All rights reserved.

Editor: Liza Miller
Illustration: Ana Djordjevic, Astound US
Photography: Sophie Scott
Design: Simon Daley

ISBN: 978 1 5263 0040 9
10 9 8 7 6 5 4 3 2 1

Wayland
An imprint of
Hachette Children's Group
Part of Hodder & Stoughton
Carmelite House
50 Victoria Embankment
London EC4Y 0DZ

An Hachette UK Company
www.hachette.co.uk
www.hachettechildrens.co.uk

Printed in China

The website addresses (URLs) included in this
book were valid at the time of going to press.
However, it is possible that contents or addresses
may have changed since the publication of this
book. No responsibility for any such changes can
be accepted by either the author or the Publisher.

The Publisher would like to thank the following
for permission to reproduce their pictures.
Via Shutterstock: p 21 Melica.

FSC
www.fsc.org
MIX
Paper from
responsible sources
FSC® C104740